CW00959339

Greater SCOTTSDALE

JERRY SIEVE

AMERICAN & WORLD GEOGRAPHIC PUBLISHING

Text pages 7-68 © 1994 William Franklin
Text pages 71-106 © 1994 Alan Korwin
© 1994 American & World Geographic
Publishing, Inc.

This book may not be reproduced in
whole or in part by any means (with
the exception of short quotes for the
purpose of review) without the permis-
sion of the publisher.

Write for our catalog:
American & World Geographic
Publishing, P.O. Box 5630, Helena,
MT 59604.
Printed in the U.S.A.

Library of Congress Cataloging-in-Publication Data
Korwin, Alan.
  Scottsdale/ by Alan Korwin & William Franklin.
    p.   cm.
  Includes bibliographical references and index.
  ISBN 1-56037-019-X
  1. Scottsdale (Ariz.)--Geography. 2. Scottsdale (Ariz.)--
Pictorial works. I. Franklin, William, 1949-   . II. Title.
F819.S37K67   1994
917.91'73--dc20   93-39618

JERRY SIEVE

Thanks to the Arizona Historical Society, Tucson; Don Addison of Rawhide; Martha Contreras and Richard M. Carbajal, Jr., El Molino Mexican Cafe; Arthur W. DeCabooter, President, Scottsdale Community College; Herbert R.Drinkwater, Mayor, Scottsdale; Joan A. Fudala, Communications Director, and Maria Pieterick, Convention and Tourism Marketing Manager, Scottsdale Chamber of Commerce; JoAnn Handley, secretary of the Scottsdale Historical Society; CC Goldwater Hedley, of the Goldwater Group; Jer Inderieden, Public Affairs Director, City of Scottsdale; Christine Keith, photojournalist; William L. Kimsey, author and historian; Suzette A. Lucas, Special Projects Director, Frank Lloyd Wright Foundation; Debbie Mitchell, Vice President, Phillips & Partners; Ann Parker, friend and writer; Joseph P. Schwan, President, Double "AA" Contractors; University of Arizona Main and Special Collections libraries; and Beth Webster, Cosanti.

JERRY SIEVE

Above: Stormy sunset near Cave Creek.
Page 1: A look at city lights, from the Pinnacle Peak area.
Page 2: The Hyatt Regency-Scottsdale. COURTESY HYATT REGENCY SCOTTSDALE RESORT AT GAINEY RANCH
Page 3: Arizona saguaro cactus blossoms.
Front cover: A glance at the city. RICK GRAETZ
Back cover: Sunset flashes a final salute behind Pinnacle Peak. JERRY SIEVE

CONTENTS

SCOTTSDALE YESTERDAY BY WILLIAM FRANKLIN

SCOTTSDALE TODAY BY ALAN KORWIN

Looking north from the summit of the Superstition Mountains, known by Spaniards as the Sierra de la Espuma, Mountains of Foam.

JOHN ANNERINO

THE LAY OF THE LAND

In the beginning, before the time of native legends and American dreams, no one was yet here to see this hallowed ground. Humans did not roam the earth. The lush desert had not yet been called Sonoran. And the valley could not possibly have been thought of as paradise. But it was just that. Because the stony silence of the crystalline air was broken only by the whirling *remolinas*, "dust devils," which spun crazily across the shimmering black lava, dancing through virgin forests of emerald-green cacti that one day would be called saguaro.

The mountains—and the violent waters they bore—knew no names. They responded to the primeval forces that created them, the cyclonic winds that sometimes tickled them. But the desert river valley many would one day come to know as home could not exist without the craggy sierras that soared above it, the miraculous waters they spawned. *Kakatak Tamai*, "Crooked-Top Mountain," was one such range; it whistled in the hot desert winds at 5,077 feet, and shadowed the long valley of Paradise—the birthplace of a future town called Scottsdale—with a wall of molten yellow rock many would mistake for gold. But once this Tertiary conflagration cooled, it became the dwelling place of the Pima deities. There was only one way for these gentle desert people to view the mountains while toiling in its somber shadows: sacred. Here in the harsh high ground of Kakatak Tamai, their ancient leader was said to seek refuge from the great flood that spilled out of the desert rivers far below. But those who followed turned to stone. And there they remain today, fossilized spirits hovering on the tortured rim of the burning sky.

From the Superstition mountain rose the Eagle; From the sluggish-moving Gila rose the Hawk... There I am running, there I am running. The Shadow of Crooked Mountain.

Pima legend from George Webb's *A Pima Remembers*

RICK GRAETZ PHOTOS

*Right: Guardian of the desert.
Below: The Northeast sector of
Scottsdale.*

No matter how it was looked at, though, no two sets of eyes would ever view this mysterious range alike, not the golden eagles that still soar above it, not the "snow-birds"—winter tourists—who peer up from their frosty beer mugs, and certainly not the heat-ravaged Spaniards who first crossed this *despoblado*, "uninhabited land," in search of the fabled Seven Cities of Gold in 1540. To those who later followed in the Spaniards' tracks, it was a great "Mountain of Foam," or *Sierra de la Espuma.* They made a map of their strange vision, and the treasure they hid in its mirage-shrouded recesses: X marked the spot. Hundreds—perhaps thousands—came searching for the Spanish gold. But as early as 1545, Pedro de Casteñeda predicted the futility of such romantic notions: "Granted that they did not find the riches of which they had been told: they did not find the next best thing—a place in which to search for them."

Above: Cholla cactus and Superstition Mountains at sunset.

DICK DIETRICH

Above: Apache Lake.

Facing page: Golden volcanic mountains, the McDowells.

DICK DIETRICH

RICK GRAETZ

Above: Roosevelt Lake from Tonto National Monument. Right: McDowell Mountain area.

Facing page: Spring wildflowers near Pinnacle Peak.

JERRY SIEVE

For just that reason, the Sierra de la Espuma was—
and still remains—a dark and blood-stained desert
ground; all 160,000 square acres of the Tonto National
Forest have officially been decreed as wilderness. Its
mazelike, dead-end canyons have for centuries "dry
gulched" the unwary ("look-alike country" survivors
swear, if you give 'em half a chance to say so). And
they're crawling with horned sidewinders, rattlesnakes
so venomous they've brought grown men to their knees
before they could unsheathe their bowies or draw their
six shooters. Add to these perils the tormented screams
of lost souls who could not, or would not, listen to the
warnings, and you'd think most would have had the
good horse sense to "stay the hell out." At last count,
51 sorry pilgrims wished they had; one by one, whether
they took a bullet in the back of the head, felt the cold
steel of a knife being slid across their throat, or pressed
their cracked lips to the mouth of a dust-filled canteen,
they breathed their last in a fruitless quest for what became the legend of the Lost Dutchman's Gold. For that
reason, the mountain once known to the Pima as
Crooked-Top has since been called Superstition.

Together with the dreaded
Superstitions, this double chain
of myth-shrouded mountains
forms a mesmerizing cyclorama
that's whispered to life each day
by the breath of the rising sun.

Rio Salado — Salt River

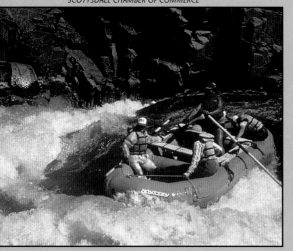

SCOTTSDALE CHAMBER OF COMMERCE

The exciting way to Roosevelt Lake.

Were it not for the lifesaving waters of the Salt River, Scottsdale and Phoenix would have dried up and blown away years ago. But this once-wild river trickles down out of the subalpine heights of 11,420-foot *dzil ligai,* "white mountain," sacred mountain of the White River Apache...and before all is said and done, plummets more than 10,000 vertical feet and drains 6,268 square miles before slaking the thirst of the desert at its palm-tree–lined trough some two hundred miles downstream.

Called the *Río de las Balsas,* "River of Rafts," by Francisco Vásquez de Coronado's men in 1540, the most famous leg of the Salt River is the 52-mile stretch that boils down Salt River Canyon, Arizona's "other Grand Canyon." White-water rafters and "hairboaters" (adventurous kayakers) alike ride turbulent spring runoff through hardtack canyon lands before bottoming out in the still waters of Roosevelt Lake. But when the Salt fills this mammoth mountain reservoir and the necklace of man-made lakes below it—an event which happens more often than city planners have a knack for predicting—the southern rim of Scottsdale and most of Phoenix takes its turn at riding out the same spring floods that first drove Pima elders to the high ground of *Kakatat Tamai.*

Time and again, news helicopters rescue stranded flat-landers who repeatedly get snookered into thinking a 4x4 pickup and a snorkel make a better way to ford a rampaging flood than a white-water raft. (In these parts, a river is called a "flood" when it has water in it.) Not to worry, though; when modern freeway bridges are put on red alert, motorists know they can always de-

DICK DIETRICH

"Hairboaters" on the Salt River.

pend on Tempe's turn-of-the-20th-century masonry bridge to get them to and from school and work, the same way settlers first relied on Hayden's Ferry there in 1879. Back then, only the Pima could speak the river's true tongue, which others have come to love and loathe in the same breath: *Onk Akimel*, "salty river." Beware.

JERRY SIEVE

Above: Continental Mountain on the city's north edge, at sunset.
Right: Hole in the Rock, thought by some to be used by the Hohokam to track the vernal equinox.

JOHN ANNERINO

But the Superstitions were not alone in creating what remains modern Scottsdale's farthest eastern vista. Shimmering in the telling distance, through incandescent waves of heat billowing off the sere desert floor, is the bold crown of the 7,903-foot Mazatzal Mountains. Together with the dreaded Superstitions, this double-chain of myth-shrouded mountains forms a mesmerizing cyclorama that's whispered to life each day by the breath of the rising sun. Thought of as impenetrable by nearly everyone except the stealthy Tonto band of Apaches who regularly traversed its tangled breach, the Superstitions and the Mazatzals still link the sluggish-moving Gila River with the forested brink of the Mogollon Rim.

Correctly pronounced "mogey-yown," and ballyhooed by such Western writers as Zane Grey, the 7,000-foot-high Mogollon Rim is a statewide precipice that forms the physiographic border between the Plateau Province to the north and the Basin and Range province to the south. Ranges like the 5,936-foot New River Mountains manage to snake their way southward out of this high country to form the northern frontier of New Scottsdale.

But it's the rivers that tumbled out of this forest-cloaked rim and surged through the cactus-studded *bajadas*, "low lands," that first brought life to what many viewed as a wasteland. On March 2, 1699, Spanish missionary and explorer Padre Eusebio Francisco Kino first described these rivers during his fifth *entrada*, or "journey," through what he called *Pimería Alta*, "Upper Piman Land." In *Luz de Tierra Incognita*, expedition diarist Captain Juan Mateo Manje wrote: "Travel-

What catch the eye are the little volcanic plugs, odd fingers of rock, cliff-terraced crags and peaks that many think of as home today.

TOM BEAN

Left: Four Peaks Mountain in the Tonto National Forest.
Below: A peek down on Paradise Valley housing.

Facing page: Desert wash near Cave Creek, Tonto National Forest. JERRY SIEVE

JOHN ANNERINO

Naming nearby Mummy
Mountain was no small
feat, either, for those bent on
maintaining the Saharan theme
for the Sonoran desert.

ing east and climbing to the top of a small mountain…
we could plainly see the Verde River which takes rise in
the land of the Apaches, running northeast to south-
east, with a grove of trees along its banks. It is joined
by another salty river [*Río Salado*, or "Salt River"], running from east to west, and the two merging together
flow in this Río Grande River [Gila River]."

What Kino possibly couldn't have imagined was that
silt from these great rivers created two fertile desert
valleys. These areas became home to a succession of
civilizations that leapfrogged from the Stone Age into
the New Age in an abrupt two centuries. Many insist
that's progress, and the *Valle de Sol*, "Valley of the
Sun," is now home to about 2.3 million people—largely
hunkered down in metropolitan Phoenix. While in the
neighboring east valley, over 185,000 folks hang their
hats and bridles in towns like Carefree, Cave Creek,
Fountain Hills, Paradise Valley, and Scottsdale, "The
West's Most Western Town."

Like the melted snow drawing from the sacred heights
of the Mazatzals and Superstitions, the Salt, Verde,
and Gila rivers have become the lifeblood of those bent
on escaping Arizona's inferno summer heat in a river
raft. Defying logic, the heat is still romanticized on
postcards and T-shirts: "Thirty miles from water, and
two feet from hell." As captivating as this wild country
might be for the distant gaze and weekend visit, the
east valley's most treasured landmarks are not the
great mountain ranges that ring it, or the rivers,
creeks, and labyrinth of canals that sustain it. Instead,
what catch the eye are the little volcanic plugs, odd fingers of rock, cliff-terraced crags and peaks that so

SCOTTSDALE HISTORICAL SOCIETY

The Sonoran desert looking south from Paradise Valley toward Camelback Mountain.

many think of as home today. That's because many east valley residents have built palatial residences as high up the burnished flanks of these desert sierras as zoning permits and homebuilding logistics will allow.

Named for Arizona's experiment to convert Arabian dromedaries to military packmules in 1856, 2,704-foot Camelback Mountain is a centerpiece for Scottsdale, Paradise Valley, and Phoenix. It was formed about the time the Colorado River first cut its teeth on the Grand Canyon 1.5 billion years ago. Hikers flee the grip of the metropolis in a thigh-burning, chest-heaving race to its

Camelback Mountain.

SCOTTSDALE HISTORICAL SOCIETY

Looking west toward Papago Buttes, when it was Papago Saguaro National Monument.

single-humped summit while climbers tempt fate, more often than their skills, in scaling the "rotten" conglomerate rock that forms the sleeping camel's head.

Naming nearby Mummy Mountain was no small feat, either, for those bent on maintaining the Saharan theme for the Sonoran desert. Forged by the same cataclysmic forces that created the camel's back, modern Mummy Mountain resembles more of an architectural launchpad for the town of Paradise Valley than the isolated 2,260-foot desert peak it once was. Palatial homes stair-step their way up its volcanic flanks.

The only landforms that look out of sorts in this sun-belt are the summits of 1,663-foot Papago Buttes. Before Congress rescinded the designation in 1930, the area was known as Papago Saguaro National Monument, for the magnificent 4,000-acre cactus plain that encircled the aboriginal landform.

Once divided from Papago Buttes, Camelback and Mummy mountains by a virgin sweep of Sonora desert, the 4,067-foot McDowell Mountains slash their way across the northeastern skyline of Scottsdale. But it's Pinnacle Peak, a dagger-sharp bone of tan granite, that draws the wandering eye, not the rugged range it spearheads. A vertical playground for ardent rock climbers, this Arizona landmark once stood sentinel over the Stoneman Wagon Road. One of the last to travel within its gnarly shadow by horse-drawn wagon was Army wife Martha Summerhayes; in 1908 she captured the sentiments of many native (and "damn-near" native) Arizonans of today: "Sometimes I hear the still voices of the Desert; they seem to be calling me through the echoes of the Past. I hear, in fancy, the wheels of an ambulance [military wagon] crunching small broken stones of the *malpais....*I hear the rattle of the ivory rings on the harness of a six-mule team...I see my white tent, so inviting after a long day's journey. But how vain those fancies! Railroad and automobile have annihilated distance, the army life of those years is past and gone, and Arizona, as we know it, has vanished from the face of the earth." The brilliant green golf courses that now encircle 3,160-foot Pinnacle Peak would not prove her wrong.

"Sometimes I hear the still voices of the Desert; they seem to be calling me through the echoes of the Past."

JOHN ANNERINO

Ancient ruins in the Superstition Mountains; the Salado people used this area circa 1100 A.D.

LOST CITIES & VANISHING PEOPLES

JOHN ANNERINO PHOTOS

Biblical drought, war, famine, earthquakes—no one knows for sure why these ancient people vanished. But long before Scottsdale billed itself as the "West's Most Western Town," with its Dodge City style storefronts, on this site stood *Pueblo Ultimo,* the Last Village. It was home to the Hohokam, or "those who have disappeared." The Last Village was not the last outpost but only one in a string of ancient Indian villages that thrived along the pulsating arteries formed by the Salt and Gila rivers.

From circa 700 to 1450 A.D., the Salt River Valley was the hub of a great native civilization that may have numbered 100,000 strong. That's because the Hohokam did what the desert people to the south couldn't do—they irrigated the desert, and they did it on a scale unparalleled in this hemisphere. Historians tell us some 300 miles of main stem *acequias*, or canals, were dug, and these ancient canal builders did it the hard way. Using crude wooden digging sticks and stone hoes, they hacked and etched trench after interconnecting trench in the burning, snake-infested black *malpais* and stone-hard *caliche*. Silver rivulets of cool water ran where no water had run before—under the flaming-yellow sun. According to Dr. O.A. Turney, all told, it's believed the Hohokam had "450,000 acres under ancient cultivation which must have supported a very large population, while up in the mountains [including Camelback] are found sacrificial caves and pueblos of stone."

Adobe pueblos, like four-story *Casa Grande* (once thought of as "America's first skyscraper"), *Los Muertos* (named "the dead" for the mummified corpses first discovered there), *Pueblo Grande, Casa Chica, Pueblo Vie-*

Top: Medicine man and woman, Melvin and Katherine Deer, reenact a sacred ceremony to ancestral Hohokam on the north end of the McDowell Mountains. Above: Metate used for grinding corn and mesquite beans (from archaeological excavations in the McDowell Mountains).

jo, clan-castles, sun temples, and ball courts—all would become models for the lavish apartment complexes and tennis courts built in this modern city 500 years after the Hohokam walked away from it all. After seven centuries of living off the salt of the earth, they disappeared. The Salt River Valley once again became the desert it always threatened to be.

Some speculated the Hohokam fled to the high ground, where visions of fertility could be realized closer to the source of the life-giving Salt. Still others said they'd gone south, as they had been doing for centuries on epic desert quests to the Gulf of California for salt and shells. Find the "Lost City," old-timers said of the rumored Hohokam village glinting in the broiling Sonoran salt pan, and you will find the answer. Someone did, around 1927, but what archaeologists later found at their ancient encampment told them only what they already suspected. The Hohokam laid over a few days in what was then, and still is, the middle of nowhere, in order to make jewelry before resuming a blistering desert trek few could survive on foot today.

Whatever happened to the "vanished ones," they left behind a system of canals so ingenious that modern settlers—frequently following the very course of these ancient waterways—could improve upon this hydrological marvel only with backhoes. (Initially, the settlers simply cleared out the ancient canals with animal and muscle power, and in the process, launched Phoenix.) But of the Hohokams' disappearance, perhaps Dr. Turney said it best: "When they forsook their last cities and left empty food chambers, all remained untouched; ollas and axes, bracelets and beads, votive and funer-

SCOTTSDALE HISTORICAL SOCIETY

Pima Indian women carrying traditional baskets.

Above: Saguaro cactus and skeletal remains of saguaro cactus stand in the desert south of Carefree.
Facing page, top left: Historic Pima dwelling near the border of Scottsdale.
Top right: Many of Scottsdale's earliest Mexican residents were laid to rest in the Camelback Cemetery—
on the opposite end of the cemetery from the anglos.
Bottom: Valley of the Sun and Camelback Mountain.

ary offerings...dedications to the ruling forces of nature; all left in vacant rooms, and all there to remain until time in slow passage had rotted roofing logs and covered them....All suffered and all became fugitives alike; the barren mountains and drought-stricken valley again became a long silent wilderness." *Pueblo Ultimo* was one such redoubt, and it disappeared without a trace in what would one day become Scottsdale.

Where the Hohokam had become masters of wild rivers, subsequent native peoples mastered hunting, gathering, and flood-water agriculture in order to eke out a living in a harsh empty ground that rarely promised paradise. The *kewevakapaya*, or southeastern band of Yavapai Indians, roamed a vast ancestral land that ranged from the cold, pine-flecked mountains of central Arizona to the burned-out, sun-scorched wastes of the lower Sonora desert. And they survived largely by collecting piñon nuts and hunting deer in the high dark forests, and harvesting saguaro fruit and slaying desert bighorn sheep in rugged sierras like the Superstitions and even Camelback Mountain. Unlike most other Arizona tribes, though, the Yavapai were not limited to a single biological life zone and because of their biodiversity, they thrived from about 1100 to 1600 A.D.

Unfortunately, however, the Yavapais' ancestral lands comprised the heart of what would become Arizona's prime real estate and during the bitter winter of 1875, they were flogged into forced relocation. Fourteen hundred captive Yavapais started out on a grueling trek from Camp Verde to the San Carlos Apache Indian Reservation "through some of the toughest territory in the

RICK GRAETZ

JERRY SIEVE

Above: Pinnacle Peak.
Left: Quartz outcrop
north of the McDowell
Mountains.

Pima Indians visited early Scottsdale in wagons.

west," wrote Sigrid Karha and Patricia Mariella in *The Fort McDowell Yavapai: A Case of Long Term Resistance to Relocation.* "Sick and old people were mercilessly left on the way to die...exhausted people were forced to cross a high running river that swept many away to their death. Food provisions were spoiled and people became ill. Stragglers were physically punished; the mutilation of some of the survivors gave testimony to such physical punishment." All because General Dudley refused to give Indian fighter General George Crook wagons for their forced relocation. "They are Indians. Let the beggars walk," Dudley told Crook.

Some Yavapai who survived moved to the Fort McDowell Indian Reservation when it was created on rich bottomlands of the Verde River in 1903 (east of present-day Scottsdale and neighboring Fountain Hills). There, they joined other tribes like the Apache, and even the Mojave, who were relocated from their own ancestral lands far to the west and east.

Believed by some to be direct descendants of the Hohokam, the Pima, on the other hand, survived largely by a digging-stick economy, frequently utilizing the same canals built by their ancestors and building small brushwork dams to impound disappearing desert run-off waters. The Pima were thought to go the enterprising Hohokam one better by farming small fertile islands of loam floating in the middle of the Gila River.

The Pimas' neighbors, the Maricopa, were linguistically related to the Yuman-speaking Mojave who dwelled along the lower Colorado River 150 miles west. It was in the direction of the setting sun that the Maricopa

JOHN ELK III

RICK GRAETZ

Above: Beavertail cactus.
Right: The Sonoran desert.

The Boulders Golf Course.

were said to travel by ancient footpath from the Salt River Valley to the Colorado River Delta in order to trade for tobacco—as if they were going to the corner store for a pack of smokes. Their tribal history was written on a calendar stick, etched with figures of horns, animals tracks, paw prints and sometimes colored notches. No doubt it included the September 1, 1857 war the Maricopa, together with the Pima, fought against hostile Quechan and Mojave who trekked 160 miles across the scorched western desert to settle the score of a centuries-old blood feud. But the Quechan and Mojave should have heeded their visions when a hawk fell dead out of the sky in front of them along the warpath; it was an omen, the elders predicted, that they would be annihilated. They were. At least 100 Mojave and Quechan slept permanently where they were slain in the pitiless desert sun.

The Pima and Maricopa's resounding victory may have been one notch on the calendar stick. Who knows how many, or what symbol was used, to record the dark memory of their mutual demise, when the great waters of the Salt and Gila were dammed and diverted away from their fertile fields at the turn of the century by the white man. For the first time in living memory, the rivers ran dry. Their natural lifeways and spiritways began to die out; age-old cultural traditions slipped away.

It's not without some irony, then, that the Pima and Maricopa now occupy two reservations that sit astride the road contoured through the Salt River Valley. Established in 1859, the 371,933-acre Gila River Reservation of the Pima sits on Interstate 10—the Golden Corridor, some call it—between Phoenix and Tucson, holding the potential of the greatest land deal in Arizona history, that is, should developers work toward the fusion of Tucson and Phoenix, built on the sites of two ancient Hohokam villages, into one super-megalopolis. Meanwhile, the 49,294-acre Salt River Indian Reservation (where both Pima and Maricopa reside) borders the deep, svelte pockets of Scottsdale: a tempting vision for developers burning to harvest touro-dollars.

It's strange, then, that native peoples like the Pima, Maricopa, Yavapai, and the dislocated Mojave and Apache, who thrived in a cruel environment the way modern peoples never would, must now rely on the same gaming devices that brought Las Vegas out of the Dark Ages. What path for survival remains, then, for these native people who were forced to adopt the strange cunning ways of displaced strangers who came beating the drums of their new civilization? Their only option may be to lease piece by precious piece the last slivers of their ancestral lands. Because, as a great Blackfoot chief spoke of Native lands far to the north of these gentle desert people, Indian country is not for sale: "Our land is more valuable than your money. It will last forever. It will not ever perish by the flames of fire. As long as the sun shines and waters flow, this land will be here to give life to man and animals. We cannot sell the lives of men and animals; therefore, we cannot sell this land" (quoted by Dee Brown in *Bury My Heart at Wounded Knee*). But the calendar-stick memory of *Pueblo Ultimo* is proof that their land may not remain in its natural state forever.

The Yavapais' ancestral lands comprised the heart of what would become Arizona's prime real estate.

JERRY SIEVE

Apache Peak sunset.

FOOL'S GOLD

JOHN ANNERINO

The vision of fat gold nuggets lured many here.

They all came looking for something: gold, glory, God. They still do—when they venture into the myth that's become Arizona, the illusion that became Scottsdale. But the fever didn't start with a German immigrant named Jacob Waltz and the legendary curse his Lost Dutchman's Gold created. The Spaniards first brought it on. The day was April 22, 1539. And the player was Fray Marcos de Niza. He was the first to cross the line (of what would later become the Arizona-Sonora border) in search of Cíbola, the fabled "seven lost cities of gold." But de Niza's guide, a black soldier of fortune named Esteban, was pole-axed by Indians upon entering the first city of gold, and de Niza had the good sense to ride hell-for-leather out of there without asking why. He made it back to Mexico with his head still intact, but the tale he wove ignited an auriferous plague that still knows no cure in these parts today.

"The cities were surrounded within walls with their gates guarded, and were very wealthy...the women wore strings of gold beads and the men girdles of gold..." claimed the Spanish adventurer. But when Francisco Vasquez de Coronado's expedition finally reached Cíbola (now thought to be in the vicinity of Zuni, New Mexico) on July 7, 1540 to confirm de Niza's incredible story, the men were not amused: "When they saw the first village, which was Cíbola, such were the curses that some hurled at Friar Marcos, that I pray God may protect him from them," wrote Pedro Castena-da de Nagera. "It is a little crowded village, looking as if it had been all crumbled together."

Delusions haven't stopped anyone since. They still keep coming, drawn to this heartless *despoblado* by dreams

There's a great stone face looking up at mine. If you pass three red hills you've gone too far. The rays of the setting sun shine upon my gold.

Jacob Waltz
(the Dutchman of the Lost Dutchman's Mine)
from his deathbed in Phoenix, October 25, 1891

only the mysterious landscape could fulfill, and only death could dispel. Most famous among them, perhaps, was Jesuit missionary Eusebio Francisco Kino. He came in search of souls, not gold, but he left a legacy that has not been equaled since. Between 1693 and 1701, the indefatigable Kino traveled an estimated 7,500 miles of unexplored trails through the harshest regions of southern Arizona and northern Sonora, and, "between baptisms, conversions, and the study of resources of the country," founded a string of Spanish missions still revered today.

Until its formative years two centuries later, though, much of Arizona's "colorful" (i.e., blood-stained) history would give the future townsite of Scottsdale a wide berth. That's because Paradise Valley had the luck of the draw in being dealt its hand north of the Salt River and east of the Verde. The routes pioneered by the dauntless Kino tended to follow the natural water courses across southern Arizona; and because they often did, they were eagerly followed by a strange procession of mountain men, immigrants, surveyors, prospectors, stage coach lines, and railroads that eventually led to the taming of the Arizona territory and the birth of Scottsdale and Phoenix.

Then, greenhorns and old hands in these parts had little choice but to follow Kino's path if they wanted a fair shake at surviving their adventure in the Arizona desert. Hammered down west of the dry line of the 100th meridian, between the 31st and 37th parallels, the Arizona territory was considered a hell on earth, stoked by furnace winds and crawling with rattlesnakes, scorpions and "savage" Indians who, many believed, would just as soon cut your heart out as not. You either crossed this deadly no-man's land, survived in it, or pushed up daisies—with or without your boots on. And Padre Kino blazed the trails many would follow.

Even ornery, trail-savvy mountain men like James Ohio Pattie followed Kino's lead along the Gila River, and because he did he came as close as any early explorer would to actually setting foot on the future townsite of Scottsdale. That's because the treasure Pattie sought also followed the rivers.

The time was 1826. Top hats were all the rage in the East. And beaver pelts were bringing $15 apiece. Profit-driven, like any good businessman, Pattie trapped up and down the Salt and Verde rivers, claiming: "In the morning of the 1st of February, we begin to ascend Black [Salt] River. We found it to abound with beavers. It is a most beautiful stream, bounded on each side with high and rich bottoms." But somewhere near the route Kino forged along the Gila River a century earlier, Pattie's expedition stumbled into some grim times, while en route to hitting the mother lode of beaver pelts on the lower Colorado River. Wrote Pattie: "We...were obliged to move slowly, as we were barefooted [having worn out their moccasins], and so having nothing to eat, we felt less the need of water. Our destitute and forlorn condition goaded us on....On the morning of the 13th, we killed a raven, which we cooked for seven men. It was unsavory flesh in itself, and would hardly have afforded a meal for one hungry man. The miserable condition of our company may be imagined when seven hungry men who had not eaten a full meal for

JOHN ANNERIN0 PHOTOS

Right: Will this marshal of Rawhide (an authentic Western town on north Scottsdale Road) have to drop some bad guys with his sawed-off shotgun before the day is through?
Below: Bronze horses, by Bob Parks, on the 5th Avenue fountain.

Facing page: The Sonoran desert.

RICK GRAETZ

ten days were all obliged to breakfast on this nauseous bird."

The forty-niners who later used the Gila Trail did not fare much better in their struggle to cross the merciless territorial desert (southwest of Scottsdale) en route to the California gold fields. Pioneered by Kino, survived by Pattie, the Gila promised water and pasturage for horses and livestock, but parties struggling along this desolate track were frequently raided by "apaches" (In territorial Arizona, terror-struck immigrants often loosely used the name "apache" to mean any group or tribe of Indians who didn't decorate the trail with rose petals every time they saw another weary procession of prairie schooners floating on the horizon.) There was a short cut (of sorts) to California's promised land and many got suckered into taking it. But so many immigrants perished on it (at least 400 during the 1850s alone), it earned the ominous name of *El Camino del Diablo*, "The Highway of the Devil."

But the terrible stories of entire families dying of dehydration didn't stop the tireless march into Arizona in quest of dreams that often became nothing more than hallucinations. Stage coach lines like the Butterfield Overland Mail carried moneyed people from the East,

The Arizona territory was considered a hell on earth, stoked by furnace winds and crawling with rattlesnakes, scorpions and "savage" Indians who, many believed, would just as soon cut your heart out as not.

It was a treasure more precious than the feverish yellow ore itself. Water.

many still sporting their beaver skin top hats. Conestoga wagons brought sodbusters. Cattle drives brought cowboys and *vaqueros*, alike; merchants divided up the beaver pelts to sell to customers. Scalawags preyed on the unwary, but they were often as unlucky. Vigilantes, reeling from pure cussedness and bad whiskey, eagerly held impromptu "necktie parties," or lynchings. Corpses swung from the big trees and turkey vultures were left with all the fixings. But nothing ever stopped the soiled doves from chasing gap-toothed miners who craved gold more than women. Yet except for Abraham Harlow Peeples—who must have been born under a lucky star for pocketing between $4,000 and $7,000 in fat gold nuggets one bloodless Arizona morning in 1862—few prospectors hit the jackpot around these parts. Those fortunes were usually reaped by mining companies, not the lone wild-eyed gold seekers who sold their souls for one last grubstake. And true, there was the Lost Dutchman's gold, the Lost Six Shooter, the *Planchas de Plata*, "Sheets of Silver," and a saddlebag of other legends that suckered tinhorns into playing deadman's poker. But the real paydirt in these parts was something altogether different. And Kino and Manje were the first to describe it, from atop that lonely desert hill on March 2, 1609. It was a treasure more precious than the feverish yellow ore itself. Water. In the desert. When bug-eyed fortune hunters first saw "the rays of the setting sun shining on this gold," they'd finally discovered Arizona's real Mother Lode. Because less than 300 years after Kino first eyeballed this treasure glimmering in the hot sand, the mesmerizing Salt River would create Arizona's own heat-warped vision of Los Angeles. It would be called Phoenix for the mythical bird that rises from its own ashes, and out of its vortex would spin a world-famous suburb called Scottsdale. But first the treasure had to be mined.

Cascading through the breach cleaving the Superstition and Mazatzal mountains fifty hard miles east of Scottsdale, the wild Salt River would not be tamed until the Italians and the Apaches joined forces in 1905. That's when construction began on Roosevelt Dam; it was the linchpin reclamation project for what politicians equated with the Second Coming for the Salt River Valley. When finally completed by Italian stone masons in 1911, it was the highest masonry dam in the world. It was a daunting 300 feet high and 110 feet wide, it cost $5.46 million to construct and it had a watershed of more than 6,000 square miles, creating a lake more than 30 miles long.

Ironically, this engineering marvel would not have been possible without the aid of the Apaches who, like Pattie, once traced the very course of the Salt River from the lofty reaches of the White Mountains. Only the Apache hadn't come in search of beaver pelts; they used the Apache Trail to raid Pima Indians a hundred years earlier. Equipped with picks and shovels, and their intimate knowledge of the terrain, they forged and chiseled a 50-mile-long mountain road atop their ancient footpath, whereby twenty-mule teams could haul men, supplies, and dynamite to the remote dam site from the last outpost and Mormon stronghold of Mesa. In *Arizona: The Wonderland*, author George Wharton James wrote that the Indians told Louis C. Hill, supervising engineer of the U.S. Reclamation Service, the following: "Tell us what you want us to do; show us how to do it; then leave us alone. We need neither bosses

LARRY ULRICH

A riot of Mexican gold poppies and blue dicks.

RICK GRAETZ

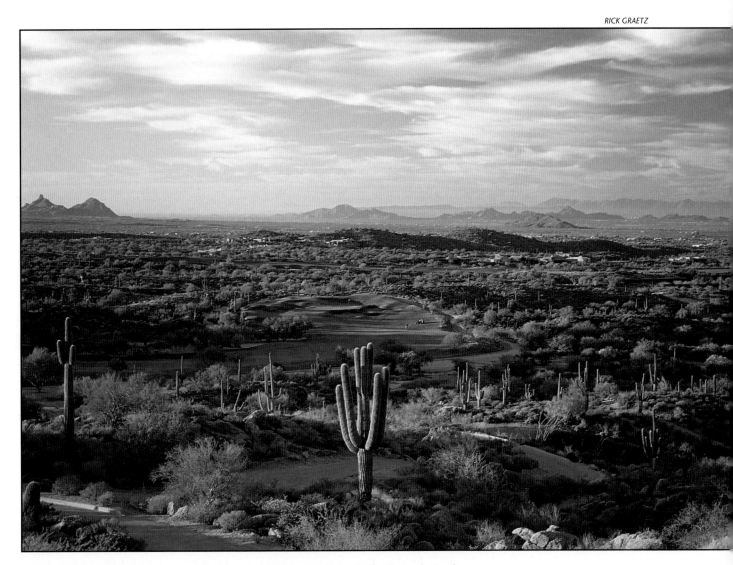

View from the Desert Mountain Clubhouse looking south towards Pinnacle Peak.

SALT RIVER PROJECT HISTORY SERVICES

Roosevelt Dam, pictured here in 1913, mined the waters that gave birth to the Salt River Valley.

nor spotters. We'll do our work faithfully and well." In a little over a year, 400 sinewy Apaches had done just that.

Rough rider turned president Theodore Roosevelt dedicated his great namesake dam in 1911, but it was George Wharton James who first foreshadowed the death of the Old West and the birth of the New West when, in 1917, he wrote: "Where the Apache used to ride in wild abandon the automobile now races, and my lady, in her silks and satins, venturing from the...ultra-civilized avenues of Eastern and Southern cities, looks out in wonderment and surprise, often in enthusiasm and delight, over scenery her eyes have never before contemplated. Here is the Arizona rarefied atmosphere, translucent, pellucid, clarified beyond anything elsewhere on earth... here are the desert and mountain colors found only in the lands of magic enchantment."

And here was the liquid gold that begat Scottsdale, Arizona, home of rarefied atmosphere for ladies dressed in silks and satins, captivated by scenery their eyes have never before seen: the luminescent, wine-red colors of the Sonoran desert and bone-hard mountains found only in this land of legend.

TOM BEAN

Trail riders in the Superstition Mountains.

GLIMPSES OF THE WAY THINGS WERE

JOHN ELK III

Eighteen eighty-eight. It is Year One—as far as the history of Scottsdale is concerned. It was the town without a past and it had a future with no name. Only the Pima knew how to eke a natural living from this dry land, hunting the fat chuckawalla lizard hurrying nowhere across the black creosote flats, and sucking the sweet blood-red juice from saguaro fruit before it exploded in the hot June sun. Pioneers in this desert knew nothing of these ways—they didn't stop long enough to ask. They only knew one direction, and they never looked back. For their progress, these strangers would have to harvest the Hohokam gold; they didn't take kindly to other ways.

Jack Swilling was the first newcomer to drink from their ancient trough. Still carrying a slug in his side from a war that claimed 600,000 lives, the ex-Johnny Reb became the "father of irrigation" in 1867. At that time he finished digging a namesake ditch that the Chamber of Commerce still claims gave birth to the mythological megalopolis that rose from the pyre of a great Native culture. Other canals, too, would trace out the last bloodlines of the Vanished Ones, in hopes of funneling off a rivulet of the liquid treasure coursing through the Salt River Valley. Between 1870 and 1878, these veins took simple names like the Tempe Canal, the Salt River Canal, the Maricopa Canal, the Grand Canal, the Mesa Canal; each of them conceived another desperate hamlet that clawed for a toehold in this hard ground. Yet if it weren't for Teddy Roosevelt riding in to save the day, they too would have disappeared like the Hohokam. But they managed to hang on long enough to follow their vision, tempered only by their lust for water, and one day became Tolleson, Glendale, Mesa, and Tempe.

The Arizona Canal under construction by William J. Murphy, "Godfather of Scottsdale."

The Arizona Canal was no different. Built by New Yorker William J. Murphy under an imposing deadline with only two hours to spare, the 35-mile-long trench was the shining path that led to the founding of Scottsdale. And Civil War chaplain Winfield Scott was one of the first to follow it. Invited to the Salt River Valley by Arizona land speculators, the visionary preacher didn't take long to realize where his greenest pastures lay. After day ten, Scott climbed off his mule, and hammered a stake in the ground on Section 23, Township 2 North, Range 4 East, calling the entire section home. Then, Scott had a good reason to call what amounted to 520 acres good. Under the Desert Land Act of March 23, 1877, homesteaders had three years to irrigate their land or turn in their chips, and it just so happened that 80 acres of the Arizona Canal slithered across the northwest corner of Scott's homestead. Paid for with four bits an acre down and another two dollars an acre to cinch the deal—$1,520 all told—his claim became the heart of Scottsdale.

Winfield Scott, his wife Helen, and his mule Maude.

SCOTTSDALE HISTORICAL SOCIETY

Like any wide-eyed land speculator in these parts, though, the good chaplain got in a little over his head, and it wasn't long before Scott started selling off parcels of paradise in order to feed the wolf scratching at the back door. Forty acres without the mule went to upstate New Yorker Mary White for $30 an acre, while over half the section was stolen by the "Godfather of Scottsdale," William J. Murphy, for $25 an acre. That left Scott with 200 acres, his pants, and Old Maude, his mule. Thus set, Scott pitched his tent on the corner of Indian School and Scottsdale roads (an area that uppity Phoenicians would later call White City for its tent-style housing of muslin hammered over orange crates). There he whiled away his retirement tending to an "orange belt" of 2,500 citrus trees and preaching the good word to faithful Baptists and Arizona lawmakers. Arizona, Scott wrote, was "the porch of perdition" and "the paradise of rattlesnakes, gila monsters, and apaches." But Scottsdale, he swore in nearly the same breath with the Bible as witness, was different.

Scott was right. As Arizona lurched for the brass ring of statehood, Phoenix was already getting crowded. Nearly 3,000 people rubbed elbows 11 miles west on a dusty dirt track while Scottsdale, a stage stop between Phoe-

Canyon Lake.

SCOTTSDALE HISTORICAL SOCIETY PHOTOS BOTH PAGES

The Little Red School House was built in 1896. Mummy Mountain can be seen on the right, and Camelback Mountain on the left.

nix and Fort McDowell, could claim only 29 residents, and half of them were ranchers and farmers. They, too, were drawn to the desert plain said by developers to be more fertile than the Nile River Valley, and for the time being they produced bumper yields of citrus and cotton. But not without grueling labor by neighboring Pima Indians (from which Arizona's cotton would take its name) and by Mexican laborers who followed the crops north. Arizona's first generation of Mexican farm workers had proud family traditions and, like the farmers' own young ones, their children needed some book learning too.

The Little Red School House was the answer. Built in 1909 for $4,500, it was a crossroads for social events, elections, and for readin', writin' and 'rithmetic—with or without the ruler cracked across knuckles. One of the first founding families to send their children there was the Corrales family; they rode hard out of the strife-stricken mining town of Cananea, Sonora—giving

The Old Mission.

birth to their son Alvaro along the way—and stayed in Scottsdale long enough to realize their dreams. Fortunately, it was a lifetime because the traditional adobe buildings the Corrales helped build are the few remaining monuments that modern Scottsdale now has to root it to its past. Using 14,000 adobe bricks from a pit near today's Center for the Arts, the Corrales built Our Lady of Perpetual Help, Scottsdale's first Catholic church, in 1933; the Old Mission, as it's fondly remembered, now serves as a symphony hall for the resident musicians. The twin-towered Jokake Inn, supposedly named from the Hopi for "mud house," on the other hand, also bears the adobe craftsmanship of Emilio and Jesus Corrales; Scottsdale's first resort, the Jokake Inn now serves as the centerpiece for the Phoenician Resort, the $330 million five-star mega-resort cleaved into the rump of Camelback Mountain astraddle the citrus-lined border of Phoenix and Scottsdale.

In a state that prides itself on conservative politics, equal rights were slow as a desert tortoise coming to this country. When the Corrales family were denied admission into one of the local greasy spoons, they had the gumption to convert their adobe pool hall into a

The Mission, once Our Lady of Perpetual Help church, was built by the Corrales family.

JOHN ANNERINO

JOHN ANNERINO

RICK GRAETZ

Above: Gainey Ranch golf course.
Top: Our Lady of Perpetual Help church today.
Left: Senita cactus and century plant. Desert Botanical Gardens.

Looking south on Brown Avenue toward J. Chew's store.

restaurant. Called *Los Olivos* for Winfield Scott's olive trees that still shade Second Street, it has become a renowned cantina for locals weaned on real Sonoran-style Mexican food, but especially for seasonal visitors who tickle their innards with icy teeth-cracking margaritas, and their toes with chile-hot salsa music.

With Mexican immigrants toiling in the fields of early Scottsdale, along with local Pimas, merchants like the J. Chew (or Ju Chu?) Song family set up shop on Brown Street in 1928 by converting another pool hall (which also doubled as a silent movie theater), into the neighborhood's second grocery store. Mrs. Song had a fondness for her faithful customers and reportedly used Chinese herbs to cure them when they were sick

The twin towers of the Jokake Inn, Scottsdale's first resort.

or injured in the fields. She soon had so many requests for items from Mexico, though, that the store slowly evolved into J. Chew's Mexican Imports. It is one of the last vestiges of old Scottsdale today.

So is Cavalliere's Blacksmith Shop. Opening it in 1910 on the outskirts of Scottsdale because Scottsdale raised such a stink, George Cavalliere shod horses, repaired wagon rims and in his heyday was said to promote fights between the Pima Pummeler and Prescott's Masked Marvel. Much to the delight of Phoenix bootleggers, cockfights also were held behind drawn shades—giving everyone a chance to pull down on some bad whiskey and ante up on bad bets.

Top: A member of the J. Chew family.
Right: Mannequin in front of the J. Chew's
Mexican Imports. The J. Chew Song family
converted a pool hall and set up shop on
Brown Avenue in 1928.

JOHN ANNERINO

Jokake Inn today.

Above: Typical tent house of the early 1900s at White City (Scottsdale and Indian School roads).
Top: The Ingleside Inn.

By 1914, however, wagons and hard times were growing out of fashion; pcople began paying a dollar a head to take the autostage from Scottsdale to Phoenix on lung-choking dirt roads. But the dust began to settle when, six years later, Scottsdale's first roads were oiled for the 500 residents who'd clambered into this rustic mirage. The reason was simple, and the future of Scottsdale—in fact, the entire frontier state of Arizona—was no better described than by newcomer George Wharton James. In 1917, he wrote:

"One winter I left New York in January where blizzards, snow, ice, sleet, and icicles had nearly frozen the marrow of my bones. I had seen hundreds, thousands of men shoveling snow out of the streets into wagons and had watched it hauled away and dumped into the river. I had been steam-heated in imagination while I shivered in reality—and to such an extent of reality that the air of houses, rooms, halls I entered seemed weighted down by the curses of ages. I had suffered from the vile ventilation that artificial heat seems to engender, and shaking the snow from my hat and overshoes, throwing the latter out of the car window when we fairly got West, I breathed a sigh of content. I was going to the wonderland of God's choice climate—Arizona—the real, modern, western Garden of Allah. In a few days I reached Phoenix and was whisked out to Ingleside [now Scottsdale]. There I shed my heavy underwear and outer clothes; dressed in the lightest possible suits, and went out bareheaded, morning, noon and night in a climate that begged us to come out in the open. It sang to us, whistled to us, cheered, encouraged, stimulated, strengthened us. We soon began to feel the increase of red corpuscles in the blood. The appetite became more

Called *Los Olivos* for Winfield Scott's olive trees that still shade Second Street, it has become a renowned cantina for locals weaned on real Sonoran-style Mexican food.

Below: Blending the new into the landscape.
Bottom:Third-generation blacksmith George Cavalliere Jr. at the historic Cavalliere's Blacksmith Shop, and some of the metal sculptures sold at the shop.

RICK GRAETZ

JOHN ANNERINO

vigorous, robust and easier-satisfied, with that following perfect digestion that the city epicure, feeding on heavy and highly seasoned foods, seldom knows. Sleep became more restful, more easily obtained and absolutely dreamless, and the morning awakening was to a richness of enjoyment, a sparkling exuberance of life that is equaled only by the linnet, the meadowlark and the mockingbird.

"Who would not enjoy changes such as this?"

JOHN ANNERINO PHOTOS

Top: Frank Lloyd Wright's Taliesin West.
Above: Built in 1892 by Frank M. Titus, the Titus House is Scottsdale's oldest building and is on the National Register of Historic Places.
Left: El Zarco—sculptor, muralist, mask maker, painter, playwright, and musician.

SCOTTSDALE HISTORICAL SOCIETY

Guy Roberts Pool Hall.

THE LIVABLE CITY

This city sings. It sings the song of Sonoran desert splendor. The lilt of an affluent American lifestyle wafts harmoniously over cactus-strewn landscape. Between the homes, around the congregating places, along the byways, the sweet music of the good life pervades Scottsdale.

Scottsdale is one of those lucky communities where climate, terrain and happenstance came together to spawn a remarkable place to call home. The city's history, though unique, hides few clues to its impending glory. From the sixty-two-hundredths of a square mile incorporated in 1951, a city of 185 square miles stands today. It stretches 32 miles from northern to southern tip, a mere two to seven miles wide. The 2,032 original inhabitants have increased to a substantial 155,000, too spread out to remotely be called teeming, on a townsite only one-third developed.

Those people and the positive attitudes they bring with them for a rich new life make all the difference. They have built the sense of community that marks most of America's great cities, and have created a physical site that is surpassed by none.

Blazing desert sunshine is the one tense chord in the symphony. For a good part of the year, the part when winter howls through the rest of North America, the Scottsdale sun delights seasonal visitors. Inevitably, though, the thermometer creeps into the three-digit range—it gets as hot as you'll ever want to know, in Scottsdale. A week's worth is a fresh experience, but if you don't like the heat you'll leave for sure after you experience a season of it. If it weren't for the periodic heat, Scottsdale would be overrun.

The positive attitudes they bring with them for a rich new life make all the difference. They have built the sense of community that marks most of America's great cities.

Right: Mexican bird-of-paradise flowers with El Pedregal shopping area in the background.
Below: Scottsdale's many galleries offer a variety of styles. George Lundeen's "Hearts on a Swing" was seen at O'Brien's on Main.

JERRY SIEVE

JOHN ANNERINO

Desert Botanical Gardens.

On the other hand, if you *like* the heat, find it exhilarating as the residents do, and can deal with dramas
like burning your hands when you open and start your
car, then, hey, this place is paradise. A sauna without
walls, the hot dry air caresses your skin, energizes your
step, and grants dazzling relief when the cool evening
falls, as it always does, once a day. As a fringe benefit,
golf balls travel better in these conditions. And you
don't have to shovel sunshine.

Were it not for the annexation of more than 100 square
miles of raw desert since 1983, the face of the city
would be largely suburban. With that additional land
came the huge tracts that now support an array of
wildlife few cities know. Families of deer venture near
the urbanized limits, along with packs of javelina, coy-
otes, jackrabbits and roadrunners in the undisturbed
rolling foothills of the north. Rattlesnakes creep, but
you must know where to look to find them. That is, un-
less you occupy a residence in the thick of this wilderness, in which case snakes are more frequent backyard

If you *like* the heat, find it exhilarating as the residents do, and can deal with dramas like burning your hands when you open and start your car, then, hey, this place is paradise.

visitors than you might care to admit…along with scorpions, lizards, tarantulas, bobcats, black widow spiders, desert tortoises and other denizens of the desert.

More obvious are red-tailed hawks circling lazily on the hot updrafts, and owls join turkey buzzards and the occasional bald eagle in eyeing the ground for a tempting morsel. More common cardinals, cactus wrens (the state bird), finches, gila woodpeckers, coveys of quail and others nest closer to the developed areas, which encroach ever deeper from the developed south to the northern expanses. Cackling grackles seem to have taken over shopping center parking lots, belligerently screeching as they vie with sparrows and doves for the odd crumb. Mockingbirds fill the air with their tuneful phrases, hummingbirds flit and dart, posing eye-to-eye with you, in their iridescence.

Here in the pristine, where the locals can quickly escape the metropolitan crunch and breathe the air of solitude, jeep-touring companies haul handfuls of visitors over jouncy rutted trails. For an out-of-town city dweller, the nothingness is novel, the freedom from civilization inspires a primal sense of awe. The driver stops, the passengers disembark onto a dusty desert roadway, and with nothing but the natural in sight, a forceful silence hammers down.

Burgeoning growth in this town—named the most livable city in America by the U.S. Conference of Mayors—threatens the very qualities that earned it the title. Hard at work, the McDowell Sonoran Land Trust strives to preserve the mountains that provide a breathtaking backdrop from all quarters of town, and form the heart of the desert experience in the top half of the tall skinny municipality.

Developers eye each patch of ground, eager to build more of the luxury homes that abound around the mountains. Zoning and preservation battles are being waged, and a balance will be struck in the near future—the fate of the city's vistas and lifestyle hanging on those results.

Driven by Scottsdale's designations as one of the top places to raise children (scholastic achievement is well above the national average) and as a leading place to retire—urban density inexorably increases. Gradually, constantly, new homes sprout—singly, in groups, and in master-planned communities—ever deeper into the desert, or thicker in the already populous areas. Studied Southwestern stucco is the style of choice, with red-tiled roofs stretching off in all directions. The "worst parts of town" are quite nice; the best parts are magnificent.

Rough-hewn beams extend from ceilings, rawhide-tied ladders lean on walls, wagon wheels and decaying relics adorn gravel-filled yards. Archways and adobe bespeak a strongly Mexican heritage, with the palette of a sunset splashed on walls. Gone are the frontier hardships, replaced with the distribution, convenience and air-conditioned comfort of modern society. Still present, though, carefully preserved in appearance, is the look of the way it was. Few residential communities lack the stucco-and-stick look. One or two stand out in requiring a greened non-Sonoran approach to landscaping and architecture.

Springtime wildflowers.

RICK GRAETZ

JOHN ANNERINO

Top: McCormick Ranch.
Above: Jerry Nelson—a developer with a
conscience, one who sees the future of Scottsdale
without trying to destroy its heritage.

Where better to build the first cluster of oases than at the foot of the area's favorite camel?

Through a magic yet to be explained, streets are spotless—yet trash crews are never seen. Oh, the trucks haul consumer trash on schedule, and road crews are always out there impeccably manicuring every roadway and side street. Much of the city has the look of a resort, coiffed and bedecked with lush xeriscape—the low-moisture plants preferred by a water-conscious desert community.

Palm trees line thoroughfares, Mexican birds-of-paradise bloom brilliantly orange-red-yellow, and the ever-present cactus in so many varieties decorates the land wherever you turn. Stately saguaros stretch to the heavens in their hundreds-of-years-old majesty. Cholla and prickly pear cactus spread unimpeded across the gravel equivalent of household lawns. Lush green grass covers sections where teams of gardeners provide the constant care required.

People point to the strict signage ordinances as a factor in the town's look. You can feel the difference as you enter the city limits and notice the visual clutter miraculously disappearing, replaced by foliage and striking architecture rarely more than a few stories high.

LIVING THE LIFE

The locals entertain a lot. Ubiquitous barbecues and pools get used all summer long, which means for seven months a year, from April to October. Weekends see residents lounging at poolside, doing yard work, bantering with friends invited over for the day or evening. In the winter, as a chilly 60°F nips at inhabitants (it's true that your blood thins after a while here) and the evenings dip down to near freezing, fireplaces fire up and the party moves inside.

Or the party moves downtown. Nightlife in the heart of the city is urbane and refined. You can dance, but for a really cooking nightclub, nearby Phoenix is the place to go. The choices in Scottsdale run from phenomenal cuisine to the arts, from shopping to gallery hopping, from film fare to people-watching in the malls. As the wind chill hits 30 below back East, expect long-lost relatives and friends to make a pilgrimage and drop by to join the celebration.

The young at heart cruise south to the pubs and clubs of Arizona State University in neighboring Tempe, or farther south to the blistering roar of dragsters, road racing and high performance boats at Firebird International Raceway, and the amphitheater entertainment at adjacent Compton Terrace. Head due west for Indy cars and more at Phoenix International Raceway or the Blockbuster Desert Sky Pavilion with its seasonal outdoor schedules of top entertainment. Adjacent Phoenix is the destination of choice for arena sports, dog and horse racing, concerts of every description and revelry at the hotter hot spots into the wee hours. You don't have to live in the big city to enjoy its benefits.

Scottsdale's idea of a big evening is elegant dining, live theater or a refined concert, multiplex movie theaters with plush rocking seats, a comedy club or jazz pianist, and, generally, a reasonably early return. Partying till dawn is definitely not the city's hallmark, although it has been known to occur. If the town has an official

Through a magic yet to be explained, streets are spotless—yet trash crews are never seen.

JOHN ELK III

MARY B. CORDINGLEY

Above: Scottsdale Mall fountains.
Right: Typical of Scottsdale's
classic Southwestern architecture.

RICK GRAETZ

JOHN ANNERINO

Top: Troon golf course.
Above: Many soon discovered that without water Arizona bore a striking resemblance to the haunting Spanish vision of a sand-swept despoblado, "uninhabited land," so enterprising realtors started offering—among other things—swimming pools in the desert.

food it is Southwestern cuisine, as a bit of Mexican influence rears its head at many of the finer establishments, almost regardless of their culinary bases. Mesquite-broiled anything is a tradition at many of the city's 200-plus restaurants.

AT THE CITY'S CORE

Nightlife in the heart of the city is urbane and refined.

They come from around the world to shop Scottsdale. Up there with the key streets of London, Paris and Beverly Hills is the Rodeo Drive of Southwestern haute couture, the modernized turn-of-the-century Old Town, in the heart of downtown. While the ultimate kachina doll or turquoise-and-silver bauble is not everyday fare on the Cote d'Azur, it commands its own niche here, and you'll find it in abundance. Right there alongside the potted cactus gardens, red hot salsas, Native American crafts, fine jewelry, Western wear, Mexican wares and more.

Fifth Avenue, Main Street, Marshall Way, Scottsdale Road, Brown Avenue—these streets anchor the downtown shopping district. With the greatest concentration of Southwestern and contemporary art galleries this side of the Mississippi River (well, Santa Fe has a claim to the title as well), Scottsdale is an art lover's Mecca.

The heart of the art community is at the Scottsdale Center for the Arts, completed in 1975, and operated by the Scottsdale Cultural Council with a budget of $5 million. The 82,500-square-foot facility seats 833 in the main auditorium and the Council stages over 900 cultural events annually at the Center and around town, including dance, theater, exhibitions, readings, music from the orchestral (the Center is home to the Scottsdale Symphony) to the avant garde, and even programs for kids of all ages. The Center is the focal point of the municipal mall, with city hall, the main library, the chamber of commerce and related facilities nearby. While some town centers are done up in administrative drab, the Scottsdale city complex has the look and feel of a fine commercial conference center, and serves as a site for numerous outdoor festivals year 'round.

The renowned art galleries and shops stretch out west of the mall. Thursday nights attract residents and visitors alike for popular art walks, with galleries open late and refreshments served. Some 100 galleries operate in the area—single-artist shops, sculpture, Southwestern, Native American, folk art, antiques, contemporary, eclectic mixes. Several, such as Elaine Horwitch Galleries, Suzanne Brown, Trailside, Overland, C.G. Rein and others, can turn a fair-sized museum green with envy. The big event of the year occurs in the fall, when the four-day Best of Scottsdale Art Festival commands everyone's attention. On the first Thursday after July 4, the Spectacular Summer Art Walk includes major new shows and live entertainment.

Across the great divide that is Camelback Road, the unique flavor of Old Town gives way to the world-class elegance of Fashion Square, the showpiece of Arizona malls. The anchors include Neiman Marcus and Broadway Southwest, Robinsons•May, Dillard's and Bullock's, with all the best boutique stores clustered around. The layout is long and delicious, the food court

With the greatest concentration of Southwestern and contemporary art galleries this side of the Mississippi River, Scottsdale is an art lover's Mecca.

Left: The Boulders Resort near Scottsdale.
Below: The Phoenician Resort.

COURTESY OF THE PHOENICIAN

Frank Lloyd Wright at Taliesin West in 1951.

a gourmet delight, the sheer opulence breathtaking. For food as you've never had it before try Z Tejas Grill, Aldo Baldo or P.F. Chang's China Bistro. You can walk over to Hops for a homemade brew, check out Sfuzzi for an Italian bistro, or cross the street to the party crowd at Jetz.

If you haven't dropped from shopping in the heart of town, try heading north to El Pedregal, a unique Moroccan-styled outdoor collection of stores tucked into the boulder-strewn landscape just south of the town of Carefree, which is itself worth a visit. On your way out of downtown you'll be tempted by the elegant shopping at the Borgata, with its re-created Renaissance-period Italian village architecture. For mainstream Americana superstores, try the Pavilions, recently built at the city's eastern edge on the adjoining Pima Indian reservation.

THE GOOD LIFE

In the 1990s Scottsdale landed the title of best resort destination in the country, and with good reason. No fewer than 40 resorts and hotels operate here, with 9,000 rooms and a mind-numbing list of public, private and municipal outdoor facilities: 20 golf courses, 19 driving ranges, 250 tennis courts, 21 baseball diamonds, 119 volleyball courts, 110 basketball courts and 32 soccer fields.

Five million visitors pass through annually, prompting airlines to designate inbound flights to Phoenix Sky Harbor International Airport as Phoenix/Scottsdale, despite a 17-times difference in the two cities' sizes. Europe, the Pacific Rim and points in the U.S. are the most common originations. Residents get to live in a city the world wants to visit.

That great influx contributes $1.2 billion to the economy, keeps the property taxes lower than anywhere else in the county, and helps fund the multimillion-dollar Chamber of Commerce. The Chamber, with 2,200 members and a staff of 36, is the ultimate repository of visitor and residential information.

In a class by itself, the Phoenician Resort rests in the nook of Camelback Mountain, built beyond the means of any normal for-profit enterprise. With solid marble interiors, $1.7 million in art strewn throughout, Steinway grand pianos at every turn, an eight-pool complex befitting a palace, this is the crème de la crème, with service to match. Technically in Phoenix, it enjoys a

While some town centers are done up in administrative drab, the Scottsdale city complex has the look and feel of a fine commercial conference center.

COURTESY OF THE SCOTTSDALE PRINCESS

JOHN ANNERINO

JOHN ANNERINO

Above: The Borgata, for upscale shopping.
Left: The Papago Plaza.

Facing page (top): The Scottsdale Princess Resort.
Bottom: El Pedregal, festive marketplace.

Scottsdale mailing address and is generally considered an honorary citizen.

Not to be outdone, palatial resorts such as the Scottsdale Princess, the Hyatt Regency at Gainey Ranch, the Boulders, the Marriott Mountain Shadows and others offer the finest luxury accommodations imaginable. Additional places to stay range from deluxe deluxe to the economy of Motel 6.

Tourist temptations abound. Golf addicts 100,000 strong throng to town in January to see the big names at the Phoenix Open Golf Tournament, an important stop on the PGA tour, held at the Scottsdale Tournament Players Club since 1987. The LPGA and senior PGA tourneys play here as well, in March and April respectively. The IBM/ATP Arizona Men's Tennis Championships arrives in February with its own roster of internationally recognized stars.

Rawhide, a re-created Western town nestled in the desert just north of urbanized areas, sees up to 900,000 visitors annually—second only to the Grand Canyon as an Arizona visitor attraction—and amazes them with staged gunfights, genuine stagecoaches, old-time stores, hayride dinners and a steak house straight out of the 1880s. The Pinnacle Peak Patio, a steak house farther north and deeper into the desert, can feed 1,600 at a time, and will cut off your tie and nail it to the wall if you dare walk in with one. Reata Pass serves steaks amidst the ruins of the former stage stop from Fort McDowell. Less well known in the desert stretches are places locals prefer, like Greasewood Flats and the Cowboy Cookshack, serving earthy

American chow in an environment too Western for the faint of heart.

If you can't get enough of the West, "The West's Most Western Town" stands ready to satisfy with equestrian events in perfect horse country. Some 200 miles of unpaved outdoor trails are available for riding or hiking, and horse rental firms are plentiful. The largest, WestWorld, holds nearly constant rodeos, exhibitions, polo matches, trail rides and cookouts, and is the home of the All Arabian Horse Show that attracts movie stars, equestrian aficionados, breeders and buyers from around the world in February. Four Arabian farms in Scottsdale conduct regular tours—Chauncey, Grandon, Adams and Jack Teague/2 Bits Arabian.

Also in the spring-like winter months of January and February, the Scottsdale Jaycees stage the longest horse-drawn parade in the world as part of their five-week-long Parada del Sol Rodeo and Festival. The only U.S.-sanctioned horseback mail delivery in the country arrives after the 200-mile full-gallop ride from Hol-brook, Arizona, with specially postmarked letters. Each weekend is different, with a staged horseback shootout in downtown (horses still have the right-of-way in Scottsdale), a chili cookoff, and a Professional Rodeo Cowboys Association rodeo as a wrap up.

On a more sedate note, Frank Lloyd Wright's former home and monument to human ingenuity, Taliesin West, stands to the east, in a stretch his friends thought too remote for comfort. They'll be knocking at my door soon enough, he told them, and sure enough, urban spread is at his borderlines. Along with the bur-

JOHN ANNERINO

Pinnacle Peak, above Troon Village, is a popular place to climb.

JOHN ANNERINO

*Above: A triumphant saddle bronc
at Scottsdale's Professional Rodeo
Cowboys Association rodeo.
Left: One of Scottsdale's many
professional golf tournaments.*

SCOTTSDALE CHAMBER OF COMMERCE

93

geoning housing developments, the Mayo Clinic set up shop nearby in the southern foothills of the McDowell Mountain range, linchpinning a medical community that is growing in international recognition. Scottsdale sports three major hospitals, including the world-renowned Minnesota-based facility, and is a contender to become the medical capital of the West.

Sports are not without representation here. Scottsdale Stadium, small by some standards (10,000 seats), is nonetheless the Cactus League spring training grounds for the San Francisco Giants. Nearby towns host the Milwaukee Brewers (Chandler), Seattle Mariners and San Diego Padres (Peoria), Oakland Athletics (Phoenix), Chicago Cubs (Mesa), California Angels (Tempe) and Colorado Rockies (Tucson), and they all practice against each other. The Giants' triple A minor league Firebirds play at Scottsdale Stadium from April to Labor Day.

The Arizona Cardinals football team, struggling for recognition in a league of giants, plods onward in the heat. Maybe football really does need bitter cold and snow to thrive. But that doesn't stop the Fiesta Bowl on New Year's Day, ranked one of the top five college football bowl games, invariably played in bright sun at Tempe's Diablo Stadium just south of the Scottsdale city line.

Ah, and then there are the Phoenix Suns, 1993 Western Conference Champions, defeatable only by three-peating spoilers, and then only by a lucky hoop or two. Suns' basketball games aren't just sport, they're town meetings, attracting fanatic supporters to the stunning new America West arena in downtown Phoenix for a frenzied display of Arizona patriotism.

Community sports hold a special place in town too, playing year-long through an ambitious Scottsdale recreation administration program. The city-funded events include every team sport imaginable, in an eight-park system. A whopping 95,000 catalogs are distributed quarterly, apprising taxpayers of the programs their funds support. Participation is for a nominal fee, or free. The same goes for senior programs and continuing education available to all residents. Outsiders can indulge at a slightly elevated fee.

Forty miles of paved multi-use paths serve the needs of bicyclers, joggers, roller-skaters and walkers. A good portion of these run the length of the Indian Bend Wash. This natural drainage trench used to create havoc during winter and monsoon rains twice a year, literally cutting the city in two. The Army Corps of Engineers proposed cementing the entire length into a functional storm drain. But Scottsdale does things right, and rejected that plan out of hand. Instead, the city leaders created a green belt, an award-winning engineering marvel that delights residents with recreational amenities while it's dry (most of the time) and efficiently siphons off the floods when they periodically arrive. In high water, an adventurous few will actually raft or canoe the length of the otherwise bone-dry wash!

All of this is in addition to the facilities of the Scottsdale Unified School District, with 17 elementary schools, five junior highs, four high schools and roots

With solid marble interiors, $1.7 million in art strewn throughout, Steinway grand pianos at every turn, an eight-pool complex befitting a palace, this is the crème de la crème, with service to match.

COURTESY OF THE PHOENICIAN

Above: The Phoenician golf course.
Right: Architectural detail of the Red
Lion's La Posada resort.

COURTESY OF LA POSADA

dating back to 1896. The system's 1,100 teachers work with 22,000 students. Ninety percent of Scottsdale high school graduates went on to higher education in 1993, compared to 53 percent on average across the country. Some of these go on to Scottsdale Community College, part of the second-largest community college system in the nation. The sprawling SCC campus is on Indian land at the city's eastern border.

If sports cars are your passion, you're likely to enjoy the Annual Greater Southwest Collector Car Auction (formerly the Kruse Classic Car Auction), the second-largest such event in the world. It's second only to the Barrett Jackson Auto Auction, which—you guessed it— is also held in Scottsdale, both in January. The 900 or so vehicles the auction attracts can be valued at an astounding $100 million.

When the heat gets to be too much, Scottsdalians head north to the cool upland pine forest country. Towns around the Mogollon Rim, at 5,000 feet in altitude, rarely see temperatures above 90°F, and enjoy cooling showers. If you own two homes in this state, there's a good chance one is a cabin in or around Prescott, Payson, Sedona or Flagstaff. That way, in the winter, you have a home base for skiing.

For the folks who'd rather have a boat for summer cooling, 303 lakes await. Many of the largest are within a day trip of Scottsdale, including Lake Pleasant, one of the biggest in mid-state, less than an hour away. Dams built on the life-sustaining Salt River have created Saguaro, Canyon and Apache lakes, also within easy reach. The first dam on the Salt, the one that enabled

FIREBIRDS/JESSEN ASSOCIATES

Pitcher Bob Gamez. A popular spring and summer pastime is cheering on the Firebirds at Municipal Stadium.

Pinnacle Peak Patio can feed 1,600 at a time, but they take the time to cut off your tie and nail it to the wall if you dare walk in with one.

Right: The favored shopping haunt of old-line socialites, Fashion Square. Below: The Scottsdale Princess Resort.

Facing page: In the lap of Camelback Mountain.

RICK GRAETZ

SCOTTSDALE CHAMBER OF COMMERCE

TOM BEAN

JOHN ANNERINO

the metropolitan growth of this whole area when it was completed in 1911, forms Theodore Roosevelt Lake, but is a long haul up the winding Apache Trail. One of the surprising facts Arizonans love quoting is that the state has more boats, per capita, than any other state in the union.

Aeronauts have their place in the Scottsdale sun, with hot air balloons filling the sky for a good part of the year. Powered-flight enthusiasts congregate at Scottsdale Airport, the busiest single-strip airfield in the United States, serving business and recreational fliers alike. The airport got its start as an Army Air Corps training facility in 1942, under the moniker Thunder-bird Field II. Now it supports 240,000 private takeoffs and landings annually.

Enveloping the airport is the vibrant Scottsdale Airpark, started in 1968. This 2,000-acre buffer insulates the surrounding residential areas, while providing 10,000 jobs and $1 billion in enterprise annually to the city's gross revenue base. Many relocated firms choose this location for the proximity to other businesses, available space and reasonable per-foot occupancy rates. Commuting here for residents of the northern half of town is a mere matter of minutes. The largest employer in the city is Motorola, at the southern tip of town, with a staff in excess of 4,700. The largest industry is tourism, responsible for one out of every four jobs.

The unemployment rate for Scottsdale is below the national average, hitting 4.2 in 1993. Thanks to the unflagging efforts of the well-heeled Chamber of Commerce, new businesses relocate here with remarkable frequency, attracted by the quality of life and the amenities available to employees. From 1991 to 1993, more than 30 companies moved to Scottsdale, bringing or creating more than 3,000 new jobs.

Not all comers are courted—a carefully outlined profile of high-wage–paying, clean businesses is preferred. Smokestack industries need not apply, and the incentives games played by other communities are usually not necessary in a city with so much going for it. Suits and ties are common in the workplace, but so is casual dress—a few companies demand it—and some even cel-

The Fiesta Bowl on New Year's Day is ranked one of the top five college football bowl games.

JOHN ANNERINO

Above: At home in Scottsdale.

Facing page, top: The Boulders Resort. Bottom: The world-renowned Mayo Clinic.

JOHN ANNERINO

The city leaders created a green belt, an award-winning engineering marvel that delights residents with recreational amenities.

ebrate Hawaiian Shirt Friday or some similarly light-hearted dress standard. Especially when the temperature exceeds 110°F for extended periods.

Among the Chamber's selected economic targets are service and professional businesses, technology companies (especially in computer-related fields), corporate headquarters, health care, universities and hospitality providers. Both the Arizona Innovation Network and the Arizona Technology Incubator call Scottsdale home, and for good reason. It's a great address. Intellectual, forward-thinking citizens tend to congregate here.

SCOTTSDALE'S VISION

Something about the desert lets you think. Makes you think. It has appealed to—encouraged and supported—great thinkers and the creative since biblical times. Entrepreneurs, innovators and artisans of every ilk have gravitated here, became enraptured, and stayed. Many of Scottsdale's residents learned of its treasures as chance visitors and remained to become its new human fabric.

As long ago as 1947, the privately run Chamber of Commerce was charged with the mission of making Scottsdale, "a better place to visit, meet, do business and live." They've accomplished those goals beyond their wildest dreams. Beginning in 1990 the town's leading citizens organized a series of "visioning" committees, to identify and express what the residents feel is possible and desirable for continuing the quality of life in the city.

RICK GRAETZ

Above: Looking down from Camelback Mountain.
Facing page: Celebrating early morning at Indian Bend Wash.

The visioning committees picked up the gauntlet, and their Shared Vision Report of May 1993, after 18 months of public input, identified 24 VisionTasks within four dominant themes for the town's continuing vitality: Sonoran desert, resort community, arts and culture, and health and research. Can the town's people stay true to their vision and build on past successes?

Scottsdale is now poised for a period of growth unlike anything it has known. The reputation has reached a certain critical mass. And the Seven Cs stereotype that

THE MAYOR, HERBERT R. DRINKWATER

JOHN ANNERINO

Scottsdale's award-winning flood-control parkland.

Although Scottsdale's attractiveness can be traced back to at least the 1920s, when people with breathing ailments flocked in for the hot dry air, its ascendancy to "most livable city" status (declared by the U.S. Conference of Mayors) really began in the 1980s. During this period city government was led by one man.

Herb Drinkwater came to a Scottsdale of 900 residents in August 1943, with asthma, rheumatic fever and a prognosis of one year to live. He attributed his recovery to the climate, opened up a wine and cheese business, got elected to the city council, and became mayor in 1980, a position he has held for 14 years. In typically self-effacing style, he attributes none of the city's accomplishments to himself. "It's nice to have 352 days of sunshine a year," he says, "but the warmth of Scottsdale comes from its people." The 92-percent approval rating he holds in his declared last term suggests he had at least some effect.

Having presided over the city's land annexations of the past decade, and the establishment of significant medical and resort facilities, his wish-list for the city is filling up, and he feels the need to step aside because "the facts of life are that a lot of people won't run against me, and that's not fair." His one abiding concern is to prevent unbridled growth from damaging the city he loves. "My wife always tells me she never worried about me having an affair because my affair was with Scottsdale.

"We're a victim of our own success," Drinkwater noted. "We have the weather, the friendliness, low taxes, the arts, the medical care, golf, horses, the desert...there's something for everyone here. That's what has created growth. We're a desirable place. I try to slow growth down. Quality of life is something that's hard to protect

DICK DIETRICH

Center for The Arts.

when you have people moving in faster than you can handle their needs."
What can Scottsdale do about it? "That's why we have a general plan...restrictive zoning...environmentally sensitive lands ordinance. Developers love Scottsdale, but I tell the council and the planning commission to do what's right for the city. I probably irritate one developer a day. We have to remember that not everyone can live here." Commenting on the record emigration in the 1990s he said, "Another winter like this past one, another earthquake in California, and we won't be able to stand over here." Desirable as Scottsdale is, it has its challenges mapped out.

Night lights dancing on the water.

Facing page: Desert holiday at The Foothills development. TOM BEAN

long held the state back is now officially dead; Arizona is no longer just climate, cotton, cattle, copper, citrus, cactus and cowboys.

Governor Fife Symington said, "Arizona is going to be setting standards for teamwork between business and government which the United States will be able to use as a model." Scottsdale exemplifies this paradigm. Its enlightened city government is carefully balancing the forces of development and the requirements of a superb quality of life. After all, they live here too. There's nothing to be gained by messing everything up.

For further information and up-to-the-minute details on Scottsdale attractions, call the Scottsdale Chamber of Commerce at (602) 945-8481. Ask for the *Destination Guide* and the *Scottsdale Almanac*, both gorgeous, both free.

Red Lion's La Posada Resort.

Desert Mountain golf course, looking west.

FOR FURTHER READING

Annerino, John. *Adventuring in Arizona.* Sierra Club Books, 1991.

Barnes, Will C. (Revised and Enlarged by Brad H. Granger). *Arizona Place Names.* Fascimile Ed. University of Arizona, 1985.

Bowden, Charles. *Desierto: Memories of the Future.* W.W. Norton & Company, 1991.

Bufkin, Don, and Henry P. Walker. *Historical Atlas of Arizona.* University of Oklahoma Press, 1979.

Cable, John S.; Susan L. Henry, and David E. Doyel, eds. *City of Phoenix, Archaeology of the Original Townsite.* Central Phoenix Redevelopment Agency, Phoenix, 1983.

Davis, Goode P., Jr. *Man and Wildlife in Arizona: The American Exploration Period, 1824-1865.* Arizona Fish & Game Department, Phoenix, 1986.

Ezell, Paul H. "History of the Pima." *Handbook of North American Indians: Southwest.* Vol 10. Smithsonian Institution, 1983.

Freeman, Roger and Ethel. *Dayhikes and Trail Rides in and Around Phoenix.* Gem Guide Books Co., Pico Rivera, 1988.

Hartmann, William K. *Desert Heart: Chronicles of the Sonoran Desert.* Fisher Books, Tucson, 1989.

Harwell, Henry O., and Marsha C.S. Kelly. "Maricopa." *Handbook of North American Indians: Southwest, Vol 10.* Smithsonian Institution, 1983.

James, George Wharton. *Arizona: The Wonderland.* Boston, 1917.

Khera Sigrid, and Patricia S. Mariella. "Yavapai." *Handbook of North American Indians: Southwest. Vol 10.* Smithsonian Institution, 1983.

Kimsey, Bill. *Recollections of Early Scottsdale: The Way It Was.* Bill Kimsey, Scottsdale, 1983.

Kroeber, Clifton B. and Bernard L. Fontana. *Massacre on the Gila.* University of Arizona Press, 1986.

Lynch, Richard E. *Winfield Scott: A Biography of Scottsdale's Founder.* The City of Scottsdale, 1978.

Matthews, David S. *Scottsdale: A Pictorial History of The West's Most Western Town.* David S. Matthews, Scottsdale, 1965.

Myers, Patricia Settlers. *Scottsdale: Jewel in the Desert.* Windsor Publications, 1988.

Reisner, Marc. *Cadillac Desert: The American West and Its Disappearing Water.* Penguin Press, 1986.

Roper, Thomas E. "The Historical Analysis of Scottsdale, Arizona from 1880 to 1972." *Urbanization of the American Southwest: Phoenix, Arizona 1870-1950.* Arizona State University, 1973.

Scottsdale, City of. *Indian Bend Wash.* 1985.

Swarthout, Glendon. *The Cadillac Cowboys.* O'Sullivan, Woodside & Co., Phoenix, 1975.

Turney, Dr. O.A. "Prehistoric Irrigation." *Arizona State Historian,* Vol. 2, No. 1, April 1929; No. 2, July 1929; No. 3, October 1929; No. 4, January 1930.

Webb, George. *A Pima Remembers.* University of Arizona Press, 1959.

Wyden, Peter. "The Town Millionaires Built." *Saturday Evening Post,* December 3, 1960. Vol. 233, No. 23, pp. 19-21 and 78-80.

INDEX

Italics indicate illustrations

DICK DIETRICH

Enjoying the great outdoors.

RICK GRAETZ

The Desert Mountain clubhouse is an example of the use of natural materials in harmony with the desert surroundings.